Pet
PRAYERS

SUSAN I. BUBBERS

CREATION
H O U S E
A STRANG COMPANY

PET PRAYERS by Susan I. Bubbers
Published by Creation House
A Strang Company
600 Rinehart Road
Lake Mary, Florida 32746
www.creationhouse.com

Cover design by Karen Grindley
Interior design by Jamey Money

Photos by Susan I. Bubbers and V. A. Balius

AUTHOR'S NOTE: The prayers use plural pronouns (we, our) for the pet's owners, and feminine pronouns (she, her) for the pet. You may choose to use singular or masculine pronouns where appropriate to personalize the prayers even further.

Library of Congress Control Number: 2005930407
International Standard Book Number: 1-59185-913-1

First Edition

05 06 07 08 09 — 987654321
Printed in the United States of America

Charis

In loving memory

(kare'-iss : Greek for "grace, gift"),
my close companion for many years—
soft, strong, smart, sassy,
beloved beyond words.

CONTENTS

PART 1:
STAGES OF
YOUR PET'S LIFE

Gracious Father, You know every detail of our hearts and lives. Guide us to the pet You would have us care for and love, the one who will be an addition to our family according to Your design. In Jesus' name we pray. Amen.

O LORD, You have searched me and known me.
You are intimately acquainted with all my ways.
—PSALM 139:1, 3

*Pet
Prayers*

HOMECOMING DAY
THANKSGIVING

HOMECOMING DATE:

_____

*You are a God of love and community—Father, Son,
and Holy Spirit. Thank You for adding to our home
this new pet who will contribute to our fellowship and
joy. May we also bring companionship to her and be
loving providers and protectors for her. We ask that
she relate well to all members of this household and
that she always be safe here, free from all harm, in
Jesus' name. Amen.*

God makes a home for the lonely.

PSALM 68:6

The owners may want to invite family and friends over to meet the new pet and help celebrate her arrival.

Jesus, Your name means "the Lord saves." Names are important, and we ask You to give us wisdom as we name our new pet.

At this point, the owner picks up the pet or places a hand on her head and says the following:

We name you _____ because _____. May you always prosper and be in good health among us. Amen.

Additional extemporaneous prayers may be added at this time.

The nations will see your righteousness, and all kings your glory; and you will be called by a new name which the mouth of the LORD will designate.

—ISAIAH 62:2

Holy Trinity, You exist in a perfect Trinity of Father, Son, and Holy Spirit. We pray that You would grant the grace of Your divine community to _____, _____, and_____, who live together. May they dwell in harmony and add to one another's lives. Through Jesus we pray. Amen.

Behold, how good and how pleasant it is for brothers to dwell together in unity!

—PSALM 133:1

Susan
Bubbers

Lord, we present _____ to You in this time of her youth, asking that You protect and provide for her in every way. As she grows, grant her a compliant nature and a special personality, and aid her learning. In Christ's name. Amen.

Like a shepherd He will tend His flock, in His arm He will gather the lambs and carry them in His bosom; He will gently lead the nursing ewes.
—Isaiah 40:11

To a lullaby tune; have fun improvising your own words!

Go to sleep,
    little _____.
You are so loved
    by me,
And even more
    by God above.
May He care
    for you
Night and day
Give you health
    and peace
At rest and at play.

In peace I will both lie down and sleep, for You alone, O LORD, make me to dwell in safety.
—PSALM 4:8

8

Susan Bubbers

BIRTH DATE:

_____

Lord God, You created all things, You sustain all things, and You are the Source of all life. Thank You for giving life to _____. We celebrate her life on this her _____ (number) birthday.

We celebrate the laughter, joy, and comfort that she has brought to us over this last year. We pray that You would grant her a year that is full of health, fun, peace, and safety, and give us wisdom to care for her welfare. Through Jesus Christ our Lord. Amen.

God made the beasts of the earth…and God saw that it was good.

—GENESIS 1:25

Lord, we pause today to remember Your many blessings, especially for our pet _____. Open our eyes so that we may see more and more each day the wonderful ways she comforts and encourages us. Continue to give us the grace to be diligent in her care, and help us to celebrate her life, and our own, every day. Amen.

All the people went...to celebrate a great festival, because they understood the words which had been made known to them.

—Nehemiah 8:12

At an Old Age

Susan Bubbers

Almighty and Eternal Father, You reign over all time and all things. As _____ progresses in years, grant her Your grace to have a good quality of life. Fill all her days with Your goodness and the love of her family, and establish the boundaries of her life here on earth according to Your best design. For Your name's sake we pray. Amen.

You have established all the boundaries of the earth; You have made summer and winter.
—Psalm 74:17

TERMINAL SITUATIONS

Heavenly Father, You have appointed a time for every living thing to be born and a time for every living thing to die. If this is the time for _____'s life to end here on earth, we pray You grant us the wisdom to recognize it and the grace to accept it. We place her life into Your hands, trusting in Your eternal mercy to grant her a peaceful end here and a gracious entrance into Your heavenly garden. In Jesus' name. Amen.

Big Ben, London, England

There is an appointed time for everything. And there is a time for every event under heaven—a time to give birth and a time to die; a time to plant and a time to uproot what is planted.

—ECCLESIASTES 3:1-2

Jesus, it seems this is the time for _____ to leave this world and to enter Your heavenly garden. Mercifully remove all suffering. Make the transition of death swift and full of Your peace. Usher her into Your heavenly kingdom gently and graciously. We thank You for giving her to us to share our pilgrimage here, and we look forward to being reunited with her there. _____, we love you, and we release you into your Creator's eternal hand. Go in peace. Amen.

Icon of Mary, London, England

Precious in the sight of the LORD is the death of His godly ones.

—PSALM 116:15

WHEN GRIEVING

Gracious Lord, You are able to soothe grief. Fill my mind with thoughts of the joyful life of my pet _____. Thank You for her life and all the blessings You gave me through her. I remember especially:

_____

_____

_____

Amen.

> Then I said, "It is my grief, that the right hand of the Most High has changed." I shall remember the deeds of the LORD; surely I will remember Your wonders of old.
>
> —PSALM 77:10–11

Lord God, I feel like I have a hole in my heart. My grief over the loss of _____ is so very heavy. I ask for Your strength and comfort. Please send Your Holy Spirit to help me. Amen.

> My soul weeps because of grief; strengthen me according to Your word.
>
> —PSALM 119:28

Lord Jesus, You Yourself were well acquainted with grief during Your earthly life, and You understand what I am feeling. Please come and put Your comforting arm around me and help me bear this burden. I am so thankful I do not need to go through this alone. Amen.

He was a man of sorrows and acquainted with grief.
—ISAIAH 53:3

Lord Jesus, thank You for Your promise of Eternal Life for both me and my beloved pet. I look forward to the time we will again be together in Your presence forever. Show me a glimpse even now of_____ in Your heavenly garden, full of joy and contentment. Jesus, although I am not now able to be with her, You are. Please tell her for me that I love her and miss her. And Lord, please reassure me of her state of bliss. In Your name I pray. Amen.

[Jesus said,] "Therefore you too have grief now; but I will see you again, and your heart will rejoice, and no one will take your joy away from you."
—JOHN 16:22

Part 2:
Health
and
Well-Being

Victorious Christ, You reign over all the earth, and although it is fallen, You can bring victory into it. We pray for all of Your animal kingdom, that You would provide sustenance, safety, and peace. Mercifully minimize suffering and protect life from all harm, especially from corrupt or negligent humanity.

We pray especially today for _____, that You would keep her safe and healthy, and that You would heal her of _____. In Jesus' name. Amen.

Are not five sparrows sold for two cents? Yet not one of them is forgotten before God.

—LUKE 12:6

IN TIMES OF SICKNESS

Merciful Lord, touch _____ with Your gentle hand of healing and comfort. We pray that You would supernaturally deliver her of her symptoms of _____ and heal the underlying cause of _____. We also pray that You would use veterinarians, medicines, and natural means to bring her once more to good health. Grant us wisdom and compassion as we care for her as Your stewards. In Jesus' name. Amen.

Casting all your anxiety on Him, because He cares for you.

—1 PETER 5:7

Jesus, You are near to the brokenhearted, abused, and neglected, even those who are Your creatures. This fallen world so often produces pain, which is outside Your ideal intention but not outside Your reach. You are mighty to save, and You are able to bring deliverance from the ills of this world. We earnestly pray that You would deliver _____ from all the pains of the past. Give her a new start, healing of mind and heart, and peace of soul. When needed, help her to learn to trust loving humans and to be able to find comfort in their compassion. In Christ's name. Amen.

A bruised reed He will not break, and a dimly burning wick He will not extinguish; He will faithfully bring forth justice.

—ISAIAH 42:3

Source of all life and hope, we thank You for the miracle at work in the womb of _____. We pray that You would oversee every stage of the development of her baby (or babies) and bring all through a safe delivery. In Christ's name. Amen.

Or you may pray:

Christ Jesus, You are the Lord of life, and through You all things came into being. We thank You for the new life growing in _____, who is pregnant. Nurture that life through a full term in good health. Keep _____ strong throughout her pregnancy, and may they all have a safe delivery. In Christ's name we pray. Amen.

For by Him all things were created, both in the heavens and on earth...all things have been created through Him and for Him.
—COLOSSIANS 1:16

IF LOST

Susan Bubbers

Lord of the universe, You are omnipresent and omniscient. You are everywhere, and You know all things. Watch over _____, who is away from home and lost. You are also omnipotent, all-powerful. You are able to keep her from all harm and provide for all her needs. In Your mercy, send loving people to help. Give _____ a good sense of direction. Through all these things, bring her once again home in safety. In Jesus' name. Amen.

He gives to the beast its food, and to the young ravens which cry.... Great is our Lord and abundant in strength; His understanding is infinite.

—PSALM 147:9, 5

WHEN LEFT ALONE

Loving Lord, You are limitless in Your nurture and concern for Your creation. While _____ is alone, keep her safe from every type of mishap and provide her with Your own presence for comfort. In Your mercy we pray. Amen.

For every beast of the forest is Mine, the cattle on a thousand hills. I know every bird of the mountains, and everything that moves in the field is Mine.
—PSALM 50:10–11

Every moment and every detail are in Your almighty hands, O Lord. While _____ is staying away from home, keep her in Your constant care, and provide for her safety and well-being. In Jesus' name. Amen.

My help comes from the LORD, who made heaven and earth. He will not allow your foot to slip; He who keeps you will not slumber.

—PSALM 121:2–3

WHEN TRAVELING

As we travel, we ask You, Lord Jesus, to be with us to keep us safe and prosper our journey. We pray especially for _____, that she will be peaceful and healthy throughout the trip. In Your name we pray. Amen.

The LORD, before whom I have walked, will send His angel with you to make your journey successful.
—GENESIS 24:40

Lord, You made a perfect world, but Adam's sin brought death and imperfection into it. We pray that You would be merciful and deliver us from consequences of the Fall. We ask especially for _____, who has been injured. Relieve her of any pain, and heal what has been harmed. We trust You to set all things right again in Your eternal kingdom. Amen.

Grant that Your bond-servants may speak Your word with all confidence, while You extend Your hand to heal, and signs and wonders take place through the name of Your holy servant Jesus.

—ACTS 4:29–30

[Jesus said,] "These things I have spoken to you, so that in Me you may have peace. In the world you have tribulation, but take courage; I have overcome the world."

—JOHN 16:33

PART 3:
THANKSGIVING

Jesus, You are the Prince of Peace, and You are such a Gracious Lord. We thank You for the many blessings _____ brings into our daily lives, especially for the way she _____. Grant her a joyful and compliant nature as she continues to be to us an instrument of Your blessings. In the name of the Father, and of the Son, and of the Holy Spirit. Amen.

O give thanks to the LORD, for He is good; for His lovingkindness is everlasting.

—1 CHRONICLES 16:34

THANKSGIVING FOR HEALING

Almighty Lord, You have shown Yourself faithful to heal, and You have delivered _____ from _____. We give You thanks and praise, trusting in Your continued grace to preserve her in health. In Christ's name. Amen.

Oh give thanks to the LORD, call upon His name; make known His deeds among the peoples.
—1 CHRONICLES 16:8

Lord God, You know how precious _____ is to us. We thank You for watching over her during this trip/time apart. Establish her once again in our home in peace and safety. In Your mercy we pray. Amen.

And I return to my father's house in safety, then the LORD will be my God.

—GENESIS 28:21

PART 4:
SPECIAL SCRIPTURES
AND
SERVICES

For the life of the flesh is in the blood, and I have given it to you on the altar to make atonement for your souls; for it is the blood by reason of the life that makes atonement.

—Leviticus 17:11

Animals, at least those with blood, have been given life (the word also means "soul") by God. They are not created in God's image in the way humans are, so they do not have free will that is perverted by sin and needs to be redeemed by Jesus the Savior. Animals do not have spirits and cannot be born again as humans are. However, souls have an eternal nature. Old Testament worship pointed ahead to the time One Life would be given for all, and until that time the lives of animals "postponed" judgment.

Yes, animals have a type of life that has eternally significant qualities. Therefore, we have every reason to believe that Scripture teaches that the souls of animals endure in a heavenly state in some way.

Your righteousness is like the mighty mountains, your justice like the ocean depths. You care for people and animals alike, O Lord.

—Psalm 36:6, NLT

One of the differences between animals and humanity is our ability to discern and choose between evil and good. This is one way in which humanity reflects the nature of God Himself.

> Then God said, "Let Us make man in Our image, according to Our likeness."
> —GENESIS 1:26

> He will eat curds and honey at the time He knows enough to refuse evil and choose good.
> —ISAIAH 7:15

Although God originally made everything perfect, free will got humanity into trouble. The first human chose evil, and in his choice he introduced into the spiritual DNA of humanity the corrupt sin nature. The consequences separated every person from God and eternal life.

> Therefore, just as through one man sin entered into the world, and death through sin, and so death spread to all men, because all sinned.
> —ROMANS 5:12

But God was not taken by surprise or overcome by the Fall of man. He had already prepared for it. He provided His Son, Jesus Christ, to be our Savior. Jesus came to the earth to die on the cross to pay the death penalty for sin and to rise from the dead to open for us once again the way of eternal life.

> If you confess with your mouth Jesus as Lord, and believe in your heart that God raised Him from the dead, you will be saved; for with the heart a person

believes, resulting in righteousness, and with the mouth he confesses, resulting in salvation.

—ROMANS 10:9–10

Place your faith in Jesus and be sure to share heaven with your pet.

Liturgy for the Blessing of Animals

Either a priest or layperson may officiate at this liturgy. It may be read by one person or read responsively.

Opening Acclamation

Bless the Lord, O my soul!
> O Lord my God, You are very great;
> You are clothed with splendor and majesty.

You established the earth upon its foundations, so that it will not totter forever and ever.
> You send forth springs in the valleys;
> They flow between the mountains;

They give drink to every beast of the field; the wild donkeys quench their thirst.
> Beside them the birds of the heavens dwell;
> They lift up their voices among the branches.

You water the mountains from Your upper chambers; the earth is satisfied with the fruit of Your works.

—Taken from Psalm 104

PRAYER OF THANKSGIVING

The Lord be with you.
And also with you.

Let us pray:

> *Sovereign Lord of the universe, You have revealed Your love and goodness through what You have made, through Your Word, and through Your Word made flesh, Jesus Christ, our Redeemer.*
>
> *By Him and for Him all things were created, both in the heavens and on earth. Through His life, His sacrificial death on the cross, His resurrection, and His ascension, He makes all things new. Thank You for all these blessings in Christ. Every good thing bestowed and every perfect gift is from above, coming down from You, the Father of lights.*
>
> *We give You thanks especially for the gift of creatures with which to share this life. Through them You aid, comfort, strengthen, and bring joy to our lives. Accept our praise for Your great goodness, through Jesus Christ our Lord. Amen.*
>
> —TAKEN FROM COLOSSIANS 1:16; JAMES 1:17

Let us read Genesis 1:24–31.
(Have someone read that passage of Scripture.)

The Word of the Lord
Thanks be to God.

PRAYER OF STEWARDSHIP

The Lord be with you.
And also with you.

Let us pray:

Almighty God, You have entrusted to humanity the stewardship of Your creation and all Your creatures: We ask that You would enlighten our minds with the wisdom, grace our hearts with the compassion, and enable our hands with every faculty necessary to be faithful to this task.

Manifest Your mercy in Your animal kingdom today, Lord, to protect and provide for Your creatures everywhere. Even send angels to guard them from harm and guide them to peace.

Send Your Holy Spirit, we pray, to empower us to care for Your creatures even as You care for us, knowing that we will give an account to You for all we do, through Christ our Lord. Amen.

Readings

A righteous man has regard for the life of his animal.

—PROVERBS 12:10

Each one of us shall give account of himself to God.

—ROMANS 14:12

Prayer for Blessing

Animals may now be presented for individual prayers of blessing. Scripture readings may be added between prayers.

> *Merciful Lord, we ask You to bless this animal _____ with Your divine provision and care, health and safety.*
> *May she experience love and joy even as she brings love and joy to her family, through Jesus Christ our Lord. Amen.*

Readings
    Psalm 104:18–21
    Psalm 104:24–26
    Psalm 104:27–30
    Psalm 104:31–33

The service is then concluded with the dismissal:

Let us bless the Lord.
    Thanks be to God.

At the Burial of a Pet

Burial Date:

The family chooses an appropriate place to bury the pet or urn and/or perhaps tokens of the pet's life, such as toys, blankets, pictures, etc. Different family members may be designated to read the prayers and the Scripture verses.

Gathering at the place, the family buries the pet and/or the tokens. An appropriate marker may also be put in place.

Then, the service proceeds with the following Scripture reading and prayer:

> Jesus said to her, "I am the resurrection and the life; he who believes in Me will live even if he dies."
> —John 11:25

Let us pray:

> *Heavenly Father, we believe that You have already prepared a place for _____ in Your heavenly garden. As we commit her to the ground, we believe that You have already received her soul into Your own hand. Make her transition from this life to the next a peaceful one, and lead her into the bliss of Your presence even as she is set free from the heaviness of this world. In Jesus' name we pray. Amen.*

While the following verses are read, each family member may choose to add a handful of dirt to the top of the burial site.

> Creation itself also will be set free from its slavery to corruption into the freedom of the glory of the children of God.
> —Romans 8:21